For Nevaeh
from Grandma Peggy
8/2016

Max's First Day of Preschool

Riccetti Publishing
240 Industrial Street
San Francisco, CA 94124
Copyright © 2013

Library of Congress Cataloging - in - Publication Data
Riccetti, Amanda   Max's First Day of Preschool/Amanda Riccetti
Story by Amanda Riccetti. Edited by Ryan Riccetti. Illustration and Design by Taryn Dufault.
Summary: Max embarks on his first day of preschool. Follow his journey as he meets his new teacher, new friends, and makes a special gift for his mom and dad.
ISBN 13: 978-0-615-86851-6   ISBN 10: 0-615-86851-7
[1. Preschool - Fiction. 2. Montessori - Fiction. 3. Parental Guide - Non-Fiction]

Printed in the United States

Max's First Day of Preschool

A parent and child's guide to easing the transition into preschool

Written by Amanda Riccetti

Forward

This story is dedicated to every parent who has decided to send their child, ages two and up, to preschool. In this modern day, we have become accustomed to sending our children to preschool, and I am here to reassure that you have made a great decision. Preschool is vital for your child and provides the foundation for learning that will occur later in elementary school and life.

While the idea of school may seem a bit scary for some children, most will adapt quickly and enjoy themselves. In this story, Max learns how to spend time away from his parents and build trusting relationships with adults outside his family. This will show your child how fun and safe the preschool journey is, while also demonstrating how he or she will spend time in a new environment, away from the comfort of home. When you read this story, you are preparing your child for his or her first day of preschool!

Intro

Hi there! My name is Max. I am two-and-a-half years old. Yes, I still wear diapers, but I'm honestly thinking of giving them up soon. *Shhh…* It's a secret! My mom and dad have no idea. My mom tells me I'm a big boy now, and she has to return back to work, just like my dad. This means I won't be able to stay at home with her anymore, which I'm very excited for! Playing at home or going to the park with my mom is fun, but I'm ready for a big adventure at my new preschool.

My mom and dad brought me to visit my new preschool a few weeks ago, and I got to meet a nice lady named Miss Peach, who will be my new teacher. She will be taking care of me while my mom and dad are working during the day. I think this is a great idea, and my preschool is going to be amazing! I can't wait for the wonderful playground, the huge room full of toys, and all of the other children I will become friends with. I don't think I'll ever run out of cool things to do at preschool! To all of my fellow children, once your mom and dad read you this story, you'll get to see why I was so excited for my first day of preschool.
I hope you have just as much fun as I did!

On a sunny Monday morning, Max woke up from a long night's rest.

Suddenly, he remembered that today was his first day of preschool, so he climbed out of his big boy bed, put on his slippers, and dashed over to his parent's room.

Mom was already awake, and she greeted Max at her door. With a smile, she said, "Good morning, Max! Are you excited for your first day of school?"

Max smiled at his mom and nodded his head. "Let's change your diaper and get ready for your big day," Mom said while reaching down for his hand.

Afterwards, Max and Mom went to his room to pick out what he wanted to wear for his first day of school.

Once Max was dressed, he and Mom were on their way to the kitchen for breakfast.

Mom picked Max up and placed him in his booster seat so he could have breakfast at the table.

Max watched as his dad brought breakfast to the table.
"Yum!" Max exclaimed when he saw the pancakes and strawberries.
"I hope you like them. Eat up!" said Dad.

Max was surprised because he usually ate oatmeal for breakfast.

While Mom cut his pancakes, Max asked,
"Dad, why did you make me special pancakes today?"
"To celebrate your first day at school!" Dad replied.

"The first day of school must be very special!" Max thought to himself while eating his pancakes

When breakfast was finished, Mom helped Max brush his teeth and comb his hair while Dad cleaned the kitchen.

Afterwards, Mom packed the clothes bag, and Max played with his favorite red car in the living room. It was time for Dad to leave for work, so he walked over to Max and said, "Max, have a fun day and follow all the rules at school."

Max nodded and said, "Yes, Dad!" Then, Mom walked into the living room to find Max. "It's time for us to go," she said.

Max replied, "Yes, Mom!" as he reached out his hand to take hers. It was finally time to get in the car and head off to school.

Mom opened the car door, and Max stepped in, climbed into his car seat, and "*Snap!*" went his safety straps.

Mom got in the car, buckled her seatbelt as well, turned the engine on, and "*Vroom!*"

Max was on his way to school.

As Mom drove around the corner towards the preschool, Max exclaimed, "Look Mom! It's my school!" Mom pulled up to the curb and turned off the engine.

She got out of the car, opened Max's door, and asked, "Max, are you excited for your first day at school?" as she helped him out of the car.
"Yes, Mom! I wonder what fun things I am going to do today," said Max.

Mom reached back into the car to retrieve the clothes bag and said, "Max, hold my hand so we can safely cross the street."

Max and Mom walked up to the front of the school and approached a tall door with a bell. "Mom, may I ring the bell?" Max asked.

Mom replied, "Yes, Max," as she lifted him to reach the bell. "*Buzz! Buzz! Buzz!*" Max pushed it with his little pointer finger, and the school secretary let them in.

Max got to ring the doorbell during his first day of school!

Max walked into the school and saw so many wonderful things to do! He excitedly asked, "Mom, can I go play now?"

Mom smiled and shook her head, replying, "Not yet, Max." Miss Peach, a teacher at the school, was walking over to greet Max and his mom.

Miss Peach crouched down, looked into Max's eyes, and said, "Good morning, Max! It's nice to see you again." Max smiled as Miss Peach stood up to greet his mom, "Good morning!"

Miss Peach offered her hand to Max and guided him and his mom towards the cubbies. Miss Peach showed Max his cubby and explained, "Max, this is where you keep your personal things and a change of clothes. Please remember your cubby, and look for your name tag so we won't lose any of your things."

Max looked at his cubby, looked at Miss Peach and his mom, and said, "Mom, look! This cubby has my name on it."

Max received his very own cubby during his first day of school.

Mom knew it was time for her to leave for work and allow Max a chance to get acquainted with Miss Peach and his school.

She walked Max to the playground door, kissed him goodbye on his forehead, and said, "Max, it's time for me to go to work. I love you! Listen to your teachers and have a fun day in school." Max replied, "Yes, Mom."

Miss Peach gently took Max by the hand while Mom waved goodbye. Max looked up at Miss Peach to find out what would happen next. She looked at Max, smiled, and guided him outside to the playground.

Max thought to himself, "I like Miss Peach!"

After Mom dropped Max off for his first day of school, she headed off to work and thought about him.

While sitting at her office desk, Mom thought to herself, "I wonder how Max is doing at school."

She decided to call the school and check on Max. "*Ring ring*!" The school secretary picked up the phone and responded, "Hello, you've reached Big City Montessori School. How may I help you?"

Mom answered, "Hi, this is Max's mom. I am calling to see how he is doing."
"Hello!" said the secretary. "Let me find out for you."

The secretary put Mom on hold while she went to ask Miss Peach for an update. A few minutes later, the secretary returned to the phone and reported back, "Miss Peach wants you to know Max is settling in very nicely. He seems to enjoy school and is working on a puzzle right now."

"Thank you for sharing this wonderful news," Mom responded happily.
The secretary said, "My pleasure! Call any time." Mom hung up the phone, smiled, and thought, "I'm glad Max is having a good day at school."

Mom checked on Max during his very first day of school.

Max had a very busy morning and was getting hungry! After finally becoming tired of playing, he walked over to Miss Peach and asked, "Excuse me, Miss Peach. May I have some food?"

"Max, we are going to have lunch soon. Come walk with me," Miss Peach replied.
Miss Peach walked out of the play area while holding Max's hand and announced to the other children it was time to come in and wash up for lunch.

After washing up, the children came over and sat one by one at round tables already prepared for lunch. The children politely helped serve one another during lunch: "Please pass the milk." "May I have some broccoli?" "Thank you!" said the other children.

Max was standing next to Miss Peach and wasn't sure where to sit, so he looked up and asked, "Excuse me, Miss Peach. Where may I sit?"

Miss Peach showed Max his seat and said, "Max, this is your place for lunch.
When you're done, I will take you for a short nap."

Max ate lunch during his first day of school!

When Max was finished eating, Miss Peach helped him clear his place at the lunch table. Then, she took Max by the hand and directed him over to the nap room.

When Max stepped into the room, he saw rows of cots decorated with sheets, blankets, and pillows. Max was very tired after such an exciting morning, and he was ready for his nap. Max thought to himself, "I wonder which cot is mine."

Miss Peach guided Max to a cot and said, "Max, this is your place to sleep."
Max sat down, removed his shoes, and placed his head on the pillow. Once he was comfortable, Miss Peach covered him with a blanket.

Max stretched, yawned, rolled over, and fell asleep.

Max took a nap during his first day of school!

Once Max woke up from his nap, he opened his eyes, sat up slowly, and looked around the room. "This is not my house," Max thought. Suddenly, he remembered he was still in school.

As Max was putting on his shoes, a teacher walked over and said, "Hi Max. Please come with me. I need to change your diaper and bring you back to class."

After having his diaper changed, Max went back to his classroom and decided to color a picture for Mom and Dad.

While coloring the picture, Max thought, "I love my mom and dad!"

The school day was finally coming to an end, so Miss Peach asked Max to put his work away and join the class for story time.

Miss Peach read several stories to the class and then dismissed all of the children for the day.

Max got to color pictures and enjoy story time during his first day of school!

After class was dismissed, Max continued his day in the afterschool program.

Max was in the playroom enjoying the train table, when a classmate walked over to Max and said, "Hi, my name is Jasmine! May I play with you?"

Max smiled and replied, "Yes."

Max and Jasmine played together until Jasmine's father arrived to pick her up.

Max thought to himself, "It's been a long day. I hope my mom comes to pick me up soon!"

Just as Max began to think about his mom, Miss Peach came over and said, "Max, it's time to go. Let's clean up and greet your mom!"

Miss Peach guided Max to the door, crouched down, looked Max in his eyes and said, "Max, I enjoyed taking care of you today. I'll see you tomorrow."

Mom picked Max up, gave him a big hug, and said, "Hi darling! I missed you. How was your first day?"

Max exclaimed, "It was fun!" and hugged Mom back.

It was finally time for Max to gather his belongings, so he and Mom walked
over to his cubby to get his coat.
Max started to pull the clothes bag out of his cubby, but Mom said,
"Max, please put the clothes bag back."

"Why, mom?" Max asked.
Mom looked at Max and said, "The clothes bag is for your things at school,
so we're going to leave it here in your cubby."

Max started to run down the hall. Mom called out, "Max, please remember your walking feet!"
Max slowed down, and Mom continued, "Please remember to stay close to me and not run
ahead in school. It's not safe, and it's against the rules."

"Yes, mom!" Max replied.

Mom came over, took Max by the hand, and they walked out of the school and down the street to the car.

Mom opened the car door and Max stepped in. He climbed into his car seat and "*Snap!*" went his safety straps.

Mom buckled her seatbelt, turned on the engine, and "*Vroom!*" Max was on his way back home after his first day of preschool!

Max had finally completed his first day of preschool away from Mom and Dad!

Later that night, Mom and Dad helped Max put on his pajamas for bedtime.

As he was putting on his pajamas, Max remembered he drew them each a picture during class!

Max reached into his pants pocket and pulled out two folded pieces of paper. He handed one to Mom and one to Dad. "I made this for you!" Max said with a smile.

Mom and Dad were delighted with the gifts Max made during his first day of preschool.

Finally, Mom and Dad tucked Max into his bed, read him a bedtime story, and wished him sweet dreams. Max was very tired from his big day, so he curled up, closed his eyes, and fell fast asleep.

That night, Max dreamed about all the fun he would have during his next day of preschool.

Parent Tip: Dropping Your Child Off at School

Learning to trust others in a new environment can sometimes be a long process for children. Often times, a child will experience anxiety when separating themselves from their loved ones, which can cause crying and clinginess during a drop-off. This behavior is normal and usually lasts around two to three weeks. In extreme cases, however, some children will cry every morning at drop-off, regardless of how many weeks have passed. While this may seem discouraging to parents, all of the children in these two scenarios will quickly settle down and join the program. By the time the parents arrive for pickup at the end of the day, it's apparent that all of the children have had a great day and have completely forgotten about the morning drop-off.

The children's quick transition from fear to focus after the morning drop-off highlights the parent's important role in the transition. When a parent is relaxed and leaves with positive energy, his or her child is much less likely to throw a tantrum or cling on for additional attention. It's also very beneficial for the parent to keep his or her "goodbye" short, as to not prolong the separation. For example, when a parent hangs out for a long period of time, reads stories to his or her child, or talks with other parents, the child begins to set an expectation that his or her parent will not leave. Once the parent finally decides to leave after prolonging the separation, the child will be much more likely to react negatively. Some children will even remain upset for hours before they become willing to enjoy school again.

There are several other reasons why children will cry or become clingy before their morning drop-off. Here are a few common scenarios:

• The child is not receiving enough attention before bedtime
• One of the child's parents is traveling, causing a change in the daily routine
• The child has just returned from a vacation with family

Again, the best way to avoid upsetting your child during drop-offs is to avoid "parental guilt." Turning the transition into a short, calm, and consistent routine will keep your child at ease and make him or her more confident in the long run. Lastly, if your child has had easy drop-offs in the past, but has recently begun to act out, feel free to contact your child's school. Your child may be dealing with an underlying issue and simply needs our support during that time.

For more information, please visit:
http://bigcitymontessorischool.com/resources/

About the Author

Amanda Riccetti is currently the director and owner of Big City Montessori School (BCMS) in San Francisco, CA. She is also the proud mother of two children, Robert and Jenni, and a wife to her husband, Frank. Before taking over as director and owner, Amanda began her work at BCMS in 1980 as a teacher, working hands-on with countless generations of children in the preschool program.

During Amanda's years with the school, she has been confronted by many parents who seek guidance and support while raising their children. Amanda was inspired to write a series of children's books to provide a charter for parents and a model for their children reading the books. Amanda's goal for this book series is twofold: To give parents a tool to teach their children valuable lessons, and to provide them with quick, digestible tips to guide their children through their preschool years.

In this series, Amanda purposely uses larger vocabulary, which is intended to encourage the parents and children to slow down, explain and develop a broader vocabulary, and model positive behavior. Please read this book one page at a time, stopping in between to discuss the page and allow your child to understand the lesson and connect with Max, our main character. This is a great chance to enjoy the beautiful illustrations and locate the book's hidden animal following Max throughout his preschool journey. In this book, you will find two birds following along with Max during his first preschool adventure.

This book series has also been illustrated using a more realistic style, rather than a younger, cartoon approach. Amanda strongly feels it is more respectful to the children readers and gives the story and characters a more pragmatic quality. Amanda would like to thank Taryn Dufault for her wonderful inspiration and illustrations, which have truly brought Max's world to life!